THE LONDON MIDLAND and SCOTTISH WAY

LMS Steam in the Sixties

Photographs and text by
Terence Dorrity

Irwell Press Ltd.

THE LONDON MIDLAND and SCOTTISH WAY

LMS Steam in the Sixties

Photographs and text by Terence Dorrity

I lived in Stratford-upon-Avon at the time the photographs in this book were taken. This well-known tourist town was on the ex-Great Western Railway line from Birmingham Snow Hill to Cheltenham Spa Malvern Road and from there either to South Wales via Gloucester Central station or to the West Country via Gloucester Eastgate station and Bristol Temple Meads. There was, though, a second line which crossed over the GWR one. This was the Stratford-upon-Avon and Midland Junction Railway route from Towcester to Broom Junction which was absorbed into the LMS at the 1923 grouping. Passenger services to Stratford Old Town railway station on this line had ceased in 1952 but some local pick-up goods trains, often with LMS 4F 0-6-0s in charge, and heavy freight trains going to South Wales still ran along the line. There had even been an LMS engine shed, a sub to Saltley, close by the station. It officially closed in 1957 but the water tank remained in use and the shed roads and turntable could be identified for several more years after the building was demolished. A 'new' curve linking the line to the GWR main line was opened in 1960 and was used by iron ore trains on their way to South Wales. Ex-LMS Class 5 4-6-0s and Class 8F 2-8-0s shared this traffic with BR Standard 9F 2-10-0s, ex-GWR 'Granges' and 28xx 2-8-0s and occasional WD 2-8-0s until shortly before the line was closed in July 1965. Visited by the occasional enthusiast railtour during the final years, the station also had a moment of glory because the platform was controversially resurfaced just a year before the end ready for use by the Royal Train headed by Class 5 44919 on 11 July 1964 when the Queen Mother visited Stratford-upon-Avon to officially re-open the Stratford Canal.

There were, of course, London Midland Region main line strongholds within very easy reach of Stratford. My father worked in Birmingham and I would sometimes spend a day at New Street station which was still divided by Queen's Drive between the ex-LNWR and Midland Railway platforms before it was 'modernised'. I was particularly fascinated by the Harborne Branch which was worked at the time by Johnson Midland Railway 2F 0-6-0s from Monument Lane shed. There were also visits to local Midland Region sheds, Saltley, Aston, Monument Lane, Bescot and Bushbury, as well as, in retrospect, logistically quite complicated trips. I recently found details of one of them, on Sunday 14 June 1959, when I visited Nuneaton, Stafford, Stoke, Alsager, Uttoxeter and Burton. Phew!

Rugby was a favourite spotting destination. This was principally to see LMS 'Coronation' (we called them 'Semis') and 'Princess Royal' Pacifics in action. Once there we installed ourselves on the embankment by the Clifton Road bridge within sight of the Great Central line 'Birdcage' bridge and the line to Market Harborough as well as the all important LMS West Coast Main Line. I well remember returning home on the very last regular passenger train from Rugby to the ex-LMS Leamington Spa Avenue station. It left at 7:54pm on Saturday 13 June 1959 and was pulled by Ivatt class 2 2-6-2T 41227 which had propelled the push-pull stock into Rugby on the last service in that direction. Many people turned out to mark the event and some even carried a symbolic coffin onto the train! A number of Midland Region expresses were diverted between Coventry and Rugby via Leamington Spa Avenue in the early 1960s while

'Coronation' class Pacific 46229 DUCHESS OF HAMILTON has just passed through Rugby on a Euston bound express on Thursday 19 April 1962.

electrification work was in progress on the main line. This was a rare opportunity to see 'Royal Scot', 'Jubilee' and Class 5 4-6-0s within whistling distance of 'Kings' and 'Castles'.

Another easily accessible location for me was Gloucester with its heady combination of ex-GWR and LMS main lines, depots and, of course, locomotives. Other shed visits in England ranged from Willesden and Camden in London, via Derby and Crewe, Rose Grove, Lostock Hall and Carnforth to Carlisle Kingmoor and Upperby, with many more in between. Following transfer of some lines from the Western Region to the London Midland Region the sheds local to Stratford-upon-Avon were recoded as LM depots in September 1963: Tyseley (84E) became 2A, Leamington Spa (84D) became 2L and Banbury (84C) became 2D. This change of Region allowed some steam operation to continue in the area for a little longer after the Western Region ceased its use in 1965.

I was first introduced to the ex-LMS locomotives in service in the British Railways Scottish Region in August 1963 while I waited, anxiously, for my O-level exam results. This was thanks to a week-long trip with fellow enthusiast Mike Collins armed with precious £5.5s.0d Freedom of Scotland Rail Rovers. We visited many engine sheds throughout the Region and, as there had been something of a cull of pre-grouping locomotives at the end of 1962, we found a large number of interesting engines awaiting their destiny in the shed yards. These included members of several ex-Caledonian Railway classes which had been absorbed into the LMS at the Grouping in 1923. Of particular interest were the attractive Pickersgill 72 and 113 class 4-4-0s, alas already out of use. As well as the ritual shed 'bunking', we even wrote to ask for permission to visit some depots while we were there and received the precious flimsy airmail-style paper permits 'Poste Restante' at the impressive Edinburgh General Post Office within a couple of days! Following the custom of the day, this trip involved sleeping on trains as much as possible on the longest available night run within the geographical limit of the Rover. This wasn't a problem going north but on one occasion, after oversleeping, we had to jump down onto the track at an unscheduled stop just outside Carnforth station and hitch back to Rail Rover territory at Carlisle from a roundabout on the A6 at the end of what was then called the Lancaster Bypass, one of Britain's first stretches of motorway.

A couple of years later attention had turned to the remaining ex-LNER A4s which were employed on the three-hour Aberdeen to Glasgow expresses. The LMS was represented by a handful of 'Royal Scots', Class 5s, Hughes 'Crab' 2-6-0s and Fairburn 4P 2-6-4 tank locomotives alongside the ex-LNER and Standard classes still active but an additional attraction was the use of four pre-grouping locomotives repainted in their original liveries to haul a number of special excursions. Two of these were from constituent companies of the LMS: Caledonian Railway 'Single' 123 and Highland Railway 'Jones Goods' 103. It was something of a reunion with Caledonian 123 because in 1960 there had been excited rumours among the local Stratford trainspotters to the effect that it was going to be put on display in Birmingham for a few days. Fortunately for us, this was during the week before Easter and so in the school holidays. My fellow enthusiasts and I duly caught the local train to Birmingham Moor Street station on Wednesday 13th April 1960. On arrival we found the amazing sight not only of the beautiful light blue CR 123 with its tender up against the buffers at the terminus, but also of the green ex-GWR 3440 CITY OF TRURO in front of it. In those pre-safety conscious days we were able to 'cab' both of them and even stand in front of 123's smokebox door.

There were also other memorable special trains. Midland Railway 4-4-0 1000 was out and about on the main line resplendent in Midland Railway livery for about three years from 1959. I first saw it at Aynho on the Nottingham Victoria to Oxford section of the RCTS 'East Midlander No.4' railtour on Sunday 11 September 1960 and I took a black and white photograph of it. A second chance came on Saturday 27 May 1961 when, on a Gloucestershire Railway Society special, it came through Stratford-upon-Avon. It was already getting dark and with the slow colour film then available I could only take a silhouette of it against the fading sunset. I was disappointed with the result at the time but now I rather like the photograph! I was fortunate to be on board several of the very many steam-hauled specials organised in the main by enthusiast societies. One of these was the Home Counties Railway Society 'Somerset and Dorset' tour which started from Waterloo and finished at Paddington. It ran between Bournemouth and Bath Green Park, and along the branch to Highbridge, behind ex-S&D 7F 53807 and ex-S&D 4F 44558. Another trip was an interesting combination of Midland, Eastern and Southern elements; a Warwickshire Railway Society special which visited Derby Works and shed, Doncaster Works and shed and Barrow Hill shed from Birmingham New Street behind Bulleid 'West Country' Pacific 34094 MORTEHOE. Perhaps my most intensive LMS experience at the time was on the Stephenson Locomotive Society 'Pacific Pennine Three Summits Rail Tour' which ran from Birmingham New Street over Shap to Carlisle and back via

MR 1000 passes at Aynho on the RCTS 'East Midlander No.4' tour on Sunday 11 September 1960.

53807 and 44558 on the Home Counties Railway Society 'Somerset and Dorset' special, at Highbridge on Sunday 7 June 1964.

the Settle and Carlisle line and Leeds. It was hauled by 'Coronations' 46251 CITY OF NOTTINGHAM and 46255 CITY OF HEREFORD, 'Jubilee' 45647 STURDEE and 'Royal Scot' 46155 THE LANCER. Other tours presented the opportunity for photography as the locomotives employed were usually markedly cleaner than the dwindling number still in use in daily service.

Mention of special trains would be incomplete without including the renowned 'Fifteen Guinea Special' end of steam on BR tour on Sunday 11 August 1968 which was advertised as the last steam hauled train on British Railways on standard gauge track. Much criticised at the time for the high ticket price, the 'standard gauge' reference recognised the fact that BR continued to operate steam locomotives on the 1ft 11¾ Vale of Rheidol line. It ran from Liverpool Lime Street through, very appropriately, Rainhill to Manchester Victoria and then over the Settle and Carlisle line to Carlisle. It returned by the same route. It drew large crowds eager to witness this historic last run and a very popular vantage point was, as you might expect, Ribblehead Viaduct. 45110, now preserved on the Severn Valley Railway, began the day and also had the distinction of being in charge of the final section back to Liverpool. 70013 OLIVER CROMWELL, 44871 and 44781 were also employed on the tour. This last tour had been preceded the previous weekend by as many as six 'end of steam' excursions in the north-west! It really did seem to be the end because British Railways declared a complete steam ban from the following day with the sole exception of FLYING SCOTSMAN for which the owner, Alan Pegler, had a contract permitting its use on the main line. Worse still, FLYING SCOTSMAN left for the United States the following year. We were fortunate to have the burgeoning preservation movements such as the Keighley and Worth Valley Railway, the Severn Valley Railway and the Birmingham Railway Museum at Tyseley to keep the fires of ex LMS classes lit until and beyond the moment the steam ban was lifted but it would never be quite the same again.

I had taken earlier black and white photographs with my trusty Kodak Brownie Cresta 120 roll film camera before graduating to 35mm when I obtained a Kodak Retinette. Limited colour slide film followed in 1960 when the rather slow, but I now realise colour stable over time, 12 ASA Kodachrome was the most popular brand. This was replaced by Kodachrome II and Kodachrome X with, each time, an increase in ASA speed which was obviously useful when photographing moving trains. I tried other makes in small quantities; Ilford, Perutz, High Speed Ektachrome, but relied mainly on Kodachrome and Agfa CT18. Earlier photos taken on Agfa film have lasted the fifty years or so reasonably well but some of the later ones have very annoyingly suffered badly from colour deterioration and can be grainy so have not been suitable for this book. I used the three different cameras shown in the picture over the period covered, the final one being the SLR.

Above. 46255 CITY OF HEREFORD pauses at Skipton after running along the Settle and Carlisle line on the Stephenson Locomotive Society 'Pacific Pennine Three Summits Rail Tour' on Sunday 12 July 1964.

Top right. 44871 and 44894 run along the Calder Valley near Lydgate on the Stephenson Locomotive Society (Midland Area) 'Farewell to Steam No 1' train on Sunday 4 August 1968.

CONTENTS

1: Express and Local Passenger Trains 6

2: Light Engine, Parcels and Permanent Way Trains 26

3: Delivering the Goods 31

4: Tender Locomotives on Shed 47

5: Tank Engines 72

6: Excursion Trains and Enthusiast Specials 89

7: Irish Interlude 110

8: Early Preservation 114

Fortunately, I kept detailed notes at the time I took the photographs and I found the following useful for additional information:
- The relevant British Railways London Midland Region and Scottish Region timetables.
- BR steam locomotive index: http://www.brdatabase.info
- Rail UK: http://www.railuk.info
- Six Bells Junction: The Railtour Files: http://www.sixbellsjunction.co.uk
- Warwickshire Railways: http://www.warwickshirerailways.com
- and the websites of the preserved lines mentioned.

Terence Dorrity 2021

(left) Taron Marquise 35mm camera: Taronar 1:1.8 45mm lens.
(centre) Kodak Retinette 35mm camera: Schneider-Kreuznach Reomar 1:3.5 45mm lens.
(right) Mamiya, Prismat CPH, 35mm SLR camera: Mamiya Sekor 1:1.9 48mm lens.

Copyright IRWELL PRESS LIMITED
ISBN-978-1-911262-43-5
First published in the United Kingdom in 2021
by Irwell Press Limited, 59A, High Street, Clophill,
Bedfordshire MK45 4BE
Printed by Akcent Media, UK
Tel: 01525 861888
www.irwellpress.com

1: Express and Local Passenger Trains

'Jubilee' 4-6-0 45682 TRAFALGAR passes Gloucester Horton Road shed on an express passenger train, Saturday 1 February 1964. It was built at Crewe Works and entered service in 1936. At the time of this photograph it was allocated to Bristol Barrow Road shed, from where it was withdrawn in June 1964.

45675 HARDY just north of Ashchurch station with an up express on Saturday 30 March 1963. This was just three days after the Beeching Report, 'The Reshaping of British Railways', was published. The spur to the right led to a grain store which is now the site of the Northway trading estate. St. Nicholas Church, Ashchurch, can be seen in the background. The soon-to-close branch to Evesham ran just the other side of Midland Cottage which can be seen in the trees.

Burton Black 5 44941 piloting a second locomotive and with a banker at the rear, heads north through Bromsgrove station, working hard ready to tackle the well-known two mile long Lickey Incline during the 1962/63 Winter.

Oxley Class 5 4-6-0 45263 heads south on an express at Shrewley, near Hatton, on Saturday 7 August 1965. Train 024 left Birmingham Snow Hill at 09:40 and ran via Oxford to Portsmouth Harbour where it was due to arrive at 14:23. It only ran on seven Saturdays in the summer.

Left. Camden's 'Princess Royal' Pacific 46206 PRINCESS MARIE LOUISE nears Rugby station and is about to pass under the Great Central line with the 'Mid-day Scot' on Wednesday 8 August 1962. The train had left Euston at 13:00 and was due to arrive at Glasgow Central at 20:30.

Right. 'Royal Scot' 46168 THE GIRL GUIDE heads south from Rugby on Thursday 19 April 1962. The train had through carriages from Blackpool Central, Birkenhead and Workington Main. Its finest days behind it, the engine was now at Wigan Springs Branch MPD – an outcome undreamed of when it was built at Derby in 1930 and for decades before it was withdrawn in May 1964.

Left. 46241 CITY OF EDINBURGH bound for Glasgow Central at the head of 'The Royal Scot' passes 45050 on the way to Euston on 'The Shamrock' at Rugby on Thursday 19 April 1962. 'The Royal Scot' was the 09:05 from Euston due to arrive at Glasgow Central at 16:15. 'The Shamrock' had left Liverpool at 08:10 and its expected arrival time at Euston was 12:35.

Carlisle Upperby's 46234 DUCHESS OF ABERCORN between the Great Central 'birdcage' viaduct and the A427 Clifton Road bridge at Rugby on the 'Merseyside Express' on Wednesday 8 August 1962. The train had left Southport Chapel Street at 08:50 and, non-stop from Liverpool Lime Street, was due to arrive at Euston at 13:55. 46234, which was never streamlined, was built at Crewe Works in 1938. It held the officially recorded British steam locomotive power output record, which still stands, in 1939 after it had been fitted with a double blastpipe and chimney. It was withdrawn in January 1963 and cut up at Crewe.

Just in the Welsh county of Montgomeryshire, Ivatt 2MT 2-6-0 46516 arrives at Carreghofa Halt, Llanymynech, on a local passenger train on the Llanymynech to Llanfyllin branch on Tuesday 4 August 1964. This was the 12:55 (Saturdays excepted) from Llanymynech which was due to arrive at Llanfyllin at 13:20. The short, 8½ mile branch was opened in 1863, primarily to convey limestone from the quarries. It was closed in January 1965.

Oswestry's 46516 has just left Carreghofa Halt on the local passenger train on Tuesday 4 August 1964. The picture was taken from the Ellesmere Canal and B4398 road bridge. 46516, built by BR at Swindon, entered service early in 1953 and was withdrawn in May 1967. The canal was the Llanymynech branch of the Ellesmere canal but it has now been categorised as part of the Montgomery Canal.

Class 5 45285 of Llandudno Junction near Mochdre, between Llandudno Junction and Colwyn Bay, on Thursday 1 July 1965 at the head of the 09:05 departure from Llandudno bound for London Euston, where it was due to arrive at 15:47.

Black 5 44917 rushes past at Mochdre in charge of a passenger train on Thursday 1 July 1965. The four track route has now been reduced to two tracks which were moved to allow the A55 road to be built on the old railway alignment. This 1945-built locomotive was allocated to Mold Junction at this time. It was withdrawn, from Crewe South, in November 1967 and scrapped by Cashmore's of Great Bridge.

Class 5 45345 passes under the arch at Conwy (the station was known by the Anglicised version, Conway, by British Railways at the time) heading east on the 1C91 Holyhead (depart 16:37) to Manchester Exchange (arrive 20:44) passenger train on Wednesday 30 June 1965. Built by Armstrong Whitworth in 1937, it was allocated to Holyhead shed at this time. It was withdrawn in June 1968 and scrapped by Draper's of Hull, The diesel unit in the station that can just be seen through the arch is the 16:30 Chester General to Bangor (arrive 18:18) all stations local train due to leave Conway at 17:55.

On Thursday 1 July 1965, Llandudno Junction's Class 5 45279 leaves Llandudno Junction station on the 07:40 Llandudno to Manchester Exchange (arrive 10:00) passenger train. 45279 was built by Armstrong Whitworth in 1936 and it was withdrawn in March 1968 and scrapped by Cashmores at Great Bridge.

Class 5 44810 departs Stratford-upon-Avon at 08:32 on an Evesham to Birmingham Snow Hill local train on Saturday 13 June 1964. This train was usually hauled by a 'Grange' or 'Hall' and sometimes by a 'Castle'. The line on the far right ran to an ex-Ministry of Food wartime cold store.

Dalry Road Black Five 45483 at the head of an express at Cumbernauld on Saturday 17 April 1965. The train was the 06:15 from Oban, due at Glasgow Buchanan Street at 10:28 but it was running about fifteen minutes late. This service, along the ex-Caledonian route via Callander, Dunblane and Stirling, was scheduled to be withdrawn with the closure of the line on 1 November 1965 but a landslide in Glen Ogle meant a premature end on 27 September 1965.

Class 5 45084 near Cumbernauld on Friday 16 April 1965 at the head of the 17:12 Glasgow Buchanan Street to Callander (arrive 18:35). Shedded at the time at Stirling, it was built by Vulcan Foundry at Newton-le-Willows in 1935 and withdrawn in November 1966.

Far from home, Northampton Class 5 4-6-0 44936 was at Dunblane on the 09:25 Crewe to Perth (arrive 17:00) on Saturday 10 October 1964.

Class 5 44788 starts out of Stirling station on time at 17:58 on the 17:12 Glasgow Buchanan Street to Callander passenger train on Saturday 10 October 1964. The now listed Caledonian Railway Stirling North signal box dating from 1901 is just visible to the right of the signal. The Shore Road bridge it is about to go under was replaced by the new Seaforth Bridge in 2015.

Stirling Class 5 45016 waits at Dunblane station ready to depart on the 12:22 Saturdays only 11¼ mile run to Callander (arrive 12:41) on a *dreek* 10 October 1964. It was soon to return heading the 13:30 Callander to Glasgow Buchanan Street (arrive 15:03). It was built at Crewe Works in 1935, withdrawn in July 1966 and scrapped by Arnott Young of Troon.

Stirling Black 5 45357 heads a passenger train over the River Carron on the Larbert Viaduct. It had departed from Larbert at 09:30 on the 09:17 Stirling to Edinburgh Waverley, where it was due to arrive at 10:14, on Monday 19 April 1965. The church seen through the arch is Larbert Old Parish church, built in 1820.

Shortly afterwards, Carlisle Kingmoor 'Royal Scot' 46140 THE KING'S ROYAL RIFLE CORPS crosses Larbert Viaduct with a Perth-London Euston express on Monday 19 April 1965. It was a long journey, leaving Perth at 09.00 and arriving at Euston at 19.10. 46140 was built by the North British Locomotive Company, Glasgow, in 1927 and was withdrawn in October 1965 and scrapped by J McWilliams at Shettlestone.

2: Light Engine, Parcels and Permanent Way Trains

Named after a General Manager of the London and North Western Railway, Willesden Patriot 45530 SIR FRANK REE passes by light on the now-closed Market Harborough line at Rugby on Wednesday 8 August 1962. Built at Crewe with a parallel boiler in 1933, it was rebuilt to 7P with taper boiler in 1946 and withdrawn in January 1965. It was cut up by Motherwell Machinery & Scrap at Wishaw. Originally opened by the Rugby and Stamford Railway, the line to Market Harborough closed on 6 June 1966 although the short section pictured is still in use for access to a Colas Rail depot.

Crewe South's 4F 0-6-0 44571 on a parcels train to Crewe via Market Drayton waits for the signal to depart from the down platform at Wellington at ten past seven in the morning, Saturday 15 August 1964. Wellington No.3 signal box and the Church Street bridge can be seen ahead. Behind the locomotive is ex-LMS 6-wheel 'Stove R' gangwayed guards brake van M32946M.

Saltley 4F 44226 lets off steam on a train of assorted vans and wagons on the ex-Midland down slow line near the site of the more recent Longbridge station, opened in 1978, on Saturday 11 May 1963. The houses are in Reabrook Road. It was possibly a Washwood Heath to Bromsgrove Wagon Works turn with rolling stock for repair.

Saltley 4F 0-6-0 44263, built at Derby in 1926, passing Gloucester Horton Road shed on a breakdown train on Saturday 1 February 1964. It was withdrawn from Skipton shed in May 1965 and cut up by Draper's at Hull later that year.

Saltley-based 43979 takes the ex-GWR line at Gloucester on Saturday 15 February 1964. Next to the locomotive is 1951-built 25T LowMac WP 4 wheeled low flat wagon B904553 designed to carry machinery such as what appears to be a mobile crane, possibly for permanent way work.

3: Delivering the Goods

Stanier 8F 2-8-0 48601 has just passed under the Great Central viaduct, sometimes called 'Birdcage Bridge', at Rugby on a southbound tanker train with barrier wagons on Wednesday 8 August 1962. 48601 was built at the Southern Railway Eastleigh Works in 1943. It was withdrawn in June 1965 and scrapped four months later at Cashmore's of Great Bridge.

48174 runs past 9 CANNOCK WOOD (B110) on a freight train along the ex-London and North Western Railway Rugeley-Cannock line at Hednesford on Saturday January 11 1964. This 8F had a star on its cab-side indicating that it had balanced wheelsets and motion to work at a higher speed and at the time of this photograph it was allocated to Stafford. It was withdrawn in May 1967 and scrapped at the end of that year at Cashmore's of Great Bridge. Ex-LBSCR E1 class 9 CANNOCK WOOD had arrived at the Railway Preservation Society site and was still carrying the pre-National Coal Board nationalisation letters C.R.C. (Cannock and Rugeley Collieries) on its tank sides. It was originally named BURGUNDY, with the number 110, and is now on the Isle of Wight Railway.

8F 48644 heads a mineral train along the ex-Midland Railway Birmingham-Nuneaton line near Haunchwood Colliery on Thursday 2 April 1964. The locomotive was built at the Southern Railway Brighton Works in 1943. It was based at Coalville shed at the time of the photograph. It was withdrawn in January 1966 and cut up by Cashmore's of Great Bridge. The locomotive was involved in a serious accident on 4 October 1949 when on a coal train it ran into the back of another coal train on Oakley Viaduct, near Bedford. The locomotive and fourteen wagons plunged through the parapet and fell 40 feet killing both the driver and the fireman.

44156 held at the crossing gates at Coalville Town station with a ballast train on Friday 3 January 1964. This Coalville 4F 0-6-0 entered service in 1925 and it was withdrawn the month after this photograph was taken. The line is still open for freight though the station was closed in September 1964 and demolished. The distinctive Midland tall signal box at the level crossing where High Street becomes Hotel Street on the A50 was dismantled and re-erected at the now closed Snibston Discovery Park.

Gloucester Barnwood 4F 44045 was built at Derby Works in 1925. It is seen here on a class K goods train near Horton Road Crossing, Gloucester, on Saturday 1 February 1964. It was withdrawn, from Gloucester Horton Road (85B), in November 1964 and scrapped by Cashmore's at Great Bridge.

Derby 'Jubilee' 45684 JUTLAND trundles through Gloucester Central station on a class C fully-fitted XP express goods train on Saturday 1 February 1964. It was built at Crewe Works in 1936 and withdrawn, from Bank Hall, in December 1965 and scrapped by Cashmore's at Great Bridge.

'Jubilee' 45641 SANDWICH approaches Horton Road Crossing, Gloucester, on a class H train of mineral wagons on Saturday 15 February 1964. Based at Burton at the time, it was withdrawn in September 1964 and scrapped by Cashmore's at Great Bridge.

8F 48336 of Woodford Halse nears Charwelton with an iron ore train on the Great Central on Saturday 30 January 1965. The locomotive was built at Horwich in 1943 and withdrawn in December 1967.

Another Woodford Halse 8F, 48011, heads an unfitted train of mostly empty mineral wagons at Kings Sutton on Tuesday 13 April 1965. Withdrawn in May 1967, it was scrapped by Cashmore's of Great Bridge.

Oxley's Class 5 44805 hurries past on a class C fully-fitted train of box vans, most likely containing perishable goods, near Harbury on Tuesday 13 April 1965.

Class 5 45042 hauls a class C fully-fitted freight under the Shrewley Common road bridge near Hatton station on the Great Western main line between Birmingham Snow Hill and Leamington Spa, at 12.50pm on Saturday 9 October 1965.

8F 48504 heads north with a freight at Shrewley, near Hatton, on Saturday 7 August 1965 while it was allocated to Nuneaton. It is unusually clean for the time, following a recent overhaul at Darlington, which had applied its customary 'large' numbers on the cabside. 48504 was withdrawn from Bolton in June 1968.

8F 48410 about to cross the River Avon just after passing through the ex-Stratford-upon-Avon and Midland Junction Railway Old Town station on a train of empty iron ore tipplers on Monday 28 December 1964. Although an LMS type, 48410 was one of those 8Fs built at the GWR Swindon Works, in 1943. Based at Stourbridge Junction at the time of this photograph, it was a survivor as it was not withdrawn from service until the very last month of BR steam, from Rose Grove, in August 1968. The large building behind is the now demolished government grain silo which was built next to Lucy and Nephew's mill during the Second World War.

Saltley 8F 48646 in charge of a train carrying ore and what appear to be steel billets, or blooms, bound for South Wales near Clifford Sidings on the ex-Stratford-upon-Avon and Midland Junction Railway line on Saturday 23 January 1965.

Right on the border between England and Wales, Oswestry's Ivatt 2MT 2-6-0 46512 stops for a moment at Llanymynech station on a goods train on Tuesday 4 August 1964. Although an LMS design, it was built by BR at Swindon Works in 1952. It was withdrawn in December 1966 but later bought from Woodham Bros Barry scrapyard and is now preserved on the Strathspey Railway where it has been given the name E.V.COOPER, ENGINEER. The station closed in January 1965.

Chester Midland-based Class 5 45305 approaches Llandudno Junction station from the east on a goods train. It was withdrawn in August 1968 at the very end of BR steam. It was sold to Albert Draper and Sons Ltd scrap merchants at Hull but there it was saved from the cutter's torch and it is now preserved on the Great Central Railway and carries the name ALDERMAN A. E. DRAPER.

Armstrong Whitworth-built Class 5 45376 passes by near Mochdre, between Llandudno Junction and Colwyn Bay, on a class H ballast train heading east on Thursday 1 July 1965. The diminutive Mochdre and Pabo signal box can be seen in the background. In 1860 Mochdre was the site of the first railway water troughs in the world.

Holyhead Class 5 44821 storms through the arch at Conwy (the station lies beyond) with an up cattle train (a long one, see next) on Wednesday 30 June 1965. 44821 was built at Derby Works in 1944 and withdrawn, from Crewe South, in June 1967 and scrapped by Cohens at Kettering. The arch was constructed by the Chester and Holyhead Railway in 1848 to preserve the continuous outline of the crenellated town walls.

A little later on Wednesday 30 June 1965, 44821 leaves Llandudno Junction with the cattle train, bound for the east. The impressive number of wagons means it was almost certainly one of the regular trains carrying imported Irish cattle. York was one important destination.

Hughes 'Crab' 42780 crosses Burton (sometimes referred to as Dalrymple) Viaduct with an empty coal train on the Dalmellington branch in Ayrshire on Friday 16 April 1965. The locomotive was allocated to Ayr at the time and was withdrawn later in the year, in October, to be cut up by J McWilliams at Shettlestone. Passenger services on the Dalmellington branch had ended in April the previous year but coal output at the NCB Waterside Colliery and, more recently, traffic from the Chalmerston open cast mine meant that much of the branch remained open.

4: Tender Locomotives on Shed

46225 DUCHESS OF GLOUCESTER takes coal at Willesden shed on Sunday 7 July 1963. It was built at Crewe Works and entered service in 1938 with streamlined casing which was removed in 1947. Allocated at the time of the photograph to Carlisle Upperby, it was withdrawn from there in October 1964 and scrapped by Arnott Young of Troon by the end of the year.

Left. A short time later 46225 DUCHESS OF GLOUCESTER is refuelled and ready for action at Willesden shed (1A) on Sunday 7 July 1963.

Below. 46235 CITY OF BIRMINGHAM is fully coaled at Willesden shed (1A) on Sunday 29 December 1963. It was built, streamlined, at Crewe Works in 1939. The streamlining was removed in 1946 and it was withdrawn at the end of September 1964 to be placed in the Birmingham Science Museum. Pictures of it being delivered can be found later in this book. It is now in the modern Thinktank Science Museum in Birmingham.

Left. 46252 CITY OF LEICESTER looks forlorn on Camden shed on Sunday 7 July 1963. It was built in 1942, one of the class that never appeared in streamlined form. It had been withdrawn the month before this photograph was taken and it was scrapped at Crewe later in the year. On 19 November 1951 this locomotive was involved in an accident at Polesworth, between Nuneaton and Tamworth. It had been driven at too high a speed while diverted on to a slow line at the head of the 22:00 overnight Euston-Glasgow train, overturning on its side. The carriages were derailed but remained upright and luckily there were no fatalities.

Maroon 46240 CITY OF COVENTRY stands in steam at Camden with Carlisle Upperby-based EE Type 4 (later class 40) D294 behind, on Sunday 7 July 1963. 46240 was built in 1940 as a streamlined locomotive but the casing was removed in 1947. It was withdrawn in October 1964 and scrapped by Cashmore's at Great Bridge.

Green 46255 CITY OF HEREFORD waits to take over the Stephenson Locomotive Society 'Pacific Pennine Three Summits Rail Tour' on its home shed, Carlisle Kingmoor, on Sunday 12 July 1964. Built at Crewe Works in 1946 and never streamlined; withdrawn just three months after this tour, it was scrapped by Arnott Young at Troon.

46132 THE KING'S REGIMENT LIVERPOOL stands on its home shed, Saltley, on Sunday 20 May 1962. It had been in Crewe Works the month before. This Royal Scot was built by the North British Locomotive Company at Glasgow in 1927. It was withdrawn from Carlisle Kingmoor in February 1964 and scrapped the following year by Arnott Young at Troon.

Crewe North's 46155 THE LANCER at Willesden on Sunday 7 July 1963. It was built at Derby in 1930, withdrawn from Carlisle Kingmoor in December 1964 and cut up at Arnott Young, Troon.

46200 THE PRINCESS ROYAL, in maroon but out of use, at Carlisle Upperby on Monday 26 August 1963. It had been withdrawn in November 1962 after 1½ million miles in service and was cut up by Connell's of Coatbridge in the autumn of 1964.

'Jubilee' 45577 BENGAL at its home shed Shrewsbury (6D, recoded from 89A the previous year) has just been replenished at the coaling stage on Tuesday 4 August 1964. It was built by the North British Locomotive Company, Glasgow, in 1934 and was withdrawn, from Shrewsbury, in September 1964. It was scrapped by Bird's at Morriston.

Ivatt class 4 2-6-0 43052 at Willesden shed on a murky Sunday 29 December 1963. At the time it was allocated to Crewe South. Built at Doncaster in 1950, it was withdrawn in November 1966 and scrapped by Ward's at Sheffield soon afterwards.

43000, the first Ivatt class 4 mogul, at Carlisle Kingmoor, its home shed at the time, on Sunday 12 July 1964. Built at Horwich in 1947, it was withdrawn from Blyth North in September 1967 and cut up by Clayton & Davie of Dunston-on-Tyne.

42965 waits for duty at Bushbury shed on Saturday 2 November 1963. It was one of a class of forty Stanier 2-6-0s and was built at Crewe Works as LMS 13265. These engines were given several power classifications including 6P5F but ended as 5MT. 42965 entered service in 1934 and was withdrawn in August 1964 and cut up by Cashmore's at Great Bridge. One of the class, 42968, has been preserved. Bushbury was the London and North Western Railway shed at Wolverhampton. It had been 21C until it became 2K two months before this photograph was taken.

In the 1960s as works around the country ceased steam overhauls, Swindon began taking in engines from the London Midland Region. Carrying a Nuneaton shed plate, 5E, obviously ex-works Stanier 2-6-0 42954 stands next to Heaton Mersey Ivatt 4MT 2-6-0 43120, which appears to be waiting its turn at Swindon on Sunday 20 September 1964. 42954 was built at Crewe in 1933 and 43120 at Horwich in 1951. Both were withdrawn in 1967; the Stanier in February, to be scrapped by Draper's at Hull, and the Ivatt in August to be cut up by Motherwell Machinery and Scrap at Wishaw.

Stanier 8F 2-8-0 48430 of Stourbridge Junction waits in line for action at Croes Newydd shed on Monday 11 June 1962. Built by the GWR at Swindon Works in 1944, it was withdrawn from Saltley in April 1965.

Bescot's (2F) 8F 2-8-0 48734 shows obvious fire damage at Didcot shed on Tuesday 18 August 1964. Four days earlier it had run light into an Esso Fawley-Bromford Bridge train of forty-eight petrol tank wagons at Didcot North Junction when leaving the marshalling yard near North Junction signal box. A number of tank wagons were derailed and around a dozen ended on their sides and caught fire, half melting a metal footbridge in the process. The fireman uncoupled the remaining part of the train which was hauled away. I have been told he was rewarded 10 shillings but also reprimanded for doing so and exposing himself to danger. 48734 was, as can be seen, badly damaged and on 15 October it was hauled to Crewe to be scrapped. It had been built at Darlington Works in 1945 and started life as LNER O6 class 3129.

Armstrong Whitworth-built Class 5 45305 waits for duty on Lostock Hall on Sunday 28 July 1968. It had entered service in 1937. It was apparently rostered to haul the 'Fifteen Guinea Special' BR last train on 11 August 1968 but was failed with a collapsed brick arch the previous day. It was sold for scrap to Albert Draper and Sons Ltd scrap merchants at Hull but the owner decided to preserve it. Named ALDERMAN A. E. DRAPER, it is now based on the Great Central Railway and has been used on main line excursions.

Ivatt 2-6-0 46515 at Oswestry shed, which had been 89D until it was transferred to the LMR and recoded 6E, on Tuesday 4 August 1964. 46515 was built by British Railways at Swindon in 1953 and it was withdrawn from Wigan Springs Branch in May 1967 and scrapped by Draper's of Hull. Oswestry shed was closed to steam on 18 January 1965.

'Crab' 2-6-0 42805 by the coaling stage on the ex-Glasgow and South Western Railway Ayr shed on Monday 26 August 1963. This locomotive was built at Crewe Works in 1928 as number 13105 and it was later renumbered 2805. It was withdrawn in November 1963 and scrapped by McLellan's of Langloan. A track gang can be seen working along the line.

Ex-LNWR 7F 0-8-0 48895 (still sporting LMS on its tender) on Bushbury shed on Saturday 2 November 1963. 48895 was built at Crewe Works in 1904 as Francis Webb designed LNWR B class 4-cylinder compound 1585. It was rebuilt several times, first after just over two years in 1906 as an E class 2-8-0 by George Whale, next, in 1923, it was returned to an 0-8-0 as a 2-cylinder G1 class design by Charles Bowen Cooke and then, in 1944, to its final form as a G2A, an earlier Bowen Cooke design with higher boiler pressure. It was withdrawn, from Bescot, in December 1964 and cut up by Cashmore's at Great Bridge.

Left. Officially withdrawn only a few days before, Johnson 2F 0-6-0 58148 awaits its fate at Coalville shed on Friday 3 January 1964. It had been built by Beyer Peacock as Midland Railway 1199 in 1876 and later rebuilt with a Belpaire boiler before becoming LMS 2967, later 22967, and finally BR 58148.

Below. This Johnson 2F 0-6-0, 58182, was built by Neilson and Company and entered service as Midland Railway 1242 in 1876. It became LMS 3010 and then 23010. Replaced on the Leicester West Bridge branch by more modern locomotives, it looks already out of use on Coalville shed (15E) on Friday 3 January 1964 although it was not officially withdrawn, the last of a class of 120, until the end of the month, after 87 years.

Left. Johnson 3F 0-6-0 43257 was built by Neilson & Co of Glasgow and entered service as Midland Railway 1890 in, coincidentally, 1890. It was withdrawn from Warrington Dallam in September 1962 and is seen here at Cashmore's Great Bridge scrapyard on Saturday 28 September 1963, the month before it was cut up.

Johnson 3F 0-6-0 43645 was built by the Midland Railway at Derby and entered service in 1900. At Gloucester Barnwood shed in April 1963, it had already been withdrawn for five months. It was cut up at Derby Works.

Ex-Caledonian Pickersgill 3F 300 class 0-6-0 57690 was built at St Rollox Works and entered service in 1920 as CR 677. On Saturday 24 August 1963 it is at Motherwell shed where, it will come as no surprise, much of the work involved serving the local collieries. Withdrawn just two weeks earlier, it was cut up by T.W Ward of Inverkeithing.

Drummond 294 class 'Jumbo' 2F 0-6-0 57328, also against the backdrop of the adjacent coal 'bing', on Saturday 24 August 1963. It too, is withdrawn; four months have seen the rust get hold. Built at St Rollox as CR 376 in 1891 it became LMS 17328 at the grouping. It was cut up by local firm Motherwell Machinery & Scrap of Wishaw at the end of the year.

Caledonian McIntosh 3F 0-6-0 57568 at Motherwell shed on Saturday 24 August 1963 might look ready to be dragged off for scrapping but is actually in steam and waiting for its next duty. Built by Neilson, Reid & Co in 1899 as CR 812 class 830 it was withdrawn in November 1963 and spent some time in store alongside Beattock shed before being scrapped by T.W. Ward at Inverkeithing. One of the class has been preserved, CR 828, BR 57566, at Aviemore on the Strathspey Railway.

Pickersgill 72 class 3P 4-4-0 54486 at Forfar motive power depot on Tuesday 27 August 1963. Built in 1920 at St Rollox Works as CR 81, it had been withdrawn in March 1962 and it was cut up by Arnott Young of Troon during the November after this photograph was taken. The shed, which had been 63C but was by then downgraded to a sub-shed of Perth, closed in July 1964. The building is still standing now surrounded by an industrial estate and used by G.S. Robertson and Co, steel framed building constructor.

The steaming days for Pickersgill 113 class 3P 4-4-0 54466 are over as it rests at Perth South shed (63A) on Tuesday 27 August 1963. Built at St Rollox as CR 124 in 1916, it became LMS 14466 at the grouping. It had already been withdrawn, from Aviemore, in March 1962 and it was scrapped by Motherwell Machinery & Scrap of Wishaw.

Another Caledonian 113 class 3P 4-4-0, 54465 out of action at Motherwell on Saturday 24 August 1963. Built at St Rollox as CR 121 in 1916, it became LMS 14465 at the grouping. It had been withdrawn in October 1962 and was scrapped by Motherwell Machinery & Scrap of Wishaw only a few days after this photograph was taken.

5: Tank Engines

A rather neglected looking Fairburn 4P 2-6-4T, 42239, approaches Calton Hill Tunnel in Edinburgh on Saturday 31 August 1963. It was in charge of empty stock from the Craigentinny carriage sidings to Waverley Station. 42239 was built at Derby Works and entered service in 1946. It was withdrawn in June 1964 and broken up by Motherwell Machinery & Scrap of Wishaw.

Fairburn 4P 2-6-4T 42273 arrives at Dunblane on the two coach 12 noon from Callander on Saturday 10 October 1964. Based at Dalry Road shed in Edinburgh, this locomotive was built at Derby Works in 1947, withdrawn in September 1966 and scrapped by Shipbreaking Industries at Faslane. Two of the original 277 members of this class, 42073 and 42085, have been preserved and can be seen at the Lakeside & Haverthwaite Railway in Cumbria.

Dalry Road's 42273 at work again in better weather on Monday 19 April 1965. It is crossing the River Carron on the 23-span Larbert Viaduct in charge of the 09:10 Edinburgh Waverley to Stirling (arrive 10:07) passenger train. The viaduct was opened in 1848 by the Scottish Central Railway which became part of the Caledonian Railway in 1865.

Light engine 42103 has just crossed over before reversing back under the Great Central 'Birdcage' bridge towards Rugby Station on Thursday 19 April 1962. This Fairburn 2-6-4T was built by British Railways at Brighton in 1950.

42082 had been transferred from Burton to Woodford Halse shed less than a week before it appeared on the 12:30 Banbury to Woodford Halse (arrive 12:50) local train on Thursday 15 August 1963. This service ended in June the following year.

41233 trundles along at the head of a local freight beside the tidal River Conwy on Thursday 1 July 1965. This is Llansanffraid Glan Conwy on the 27¼ mile ex-LNWR Llandudno Junction to Blaenau Ffestiniog branch. This Ivatt designed 2MT 2-6-2T was built by BR at Crewe in 1949. It was withdrawn in November 1966 and cut up by Cashmore's of Great Bridge. The line is still open to passengers and is marketed as the Conwy Valley Line.

Leamington's Ivatt 2MT 2-6-2T 41241 crosses the Stannels Bridge over the River Avon near Stratford-upon-Avon on a very short class K pick-up goods of what appears to be military material on Friday 20 March 1964. This was the Bordesley Junction to Evesham goods bound first for the Long Marston military depot on the day that the Beatles *Can't Buy Me Love* was released as a Parlophone 7" single. Withdrawn from Skipton in December 1966, it is now preserved and based on the Keighley and Worth Valley Railway.

Ivatt 2-6-2T 41230 at the Southern Region ex-London Brighton and South Coast Railway Lancing Carriage Works on 18 April 1963. It had spent its working life hitherto on the London Midland Region and was still carrying a Llandudno Junction (6G) shed plate. Alongside was one of the ex-LBSCR A1X 'Terriers', 32636, which were regularly used there. The A1X has been preserved and is to be found on the Bluebell Railway, usually in its earlier guise as 672 FENCHURCH. 41230 was withdrawn from Bournemouth in April 1967 and cut up by Cohen's of Morriston.

41270 at Bournemouth Central on Sunday 7 June 1964. 'West Country' Pacific 34102 LAPFORD is behind in the shed yard. 41270 ran on the Lymington and Swanage branches while based at Bournemouth before it was withdrawn in May 1965 and scrapped at R.S. Hayes/Bird's at Bridgend.

Deeley 0-4-0T 41528 was built at Derby Works in 1907, the first of a batch of five such tank engines. A further five were built fourteen years later. It is seen here at its home shed, Staveley Barrow Hill, on Sunday 12 May 1963. It worked at the Staveley Iron Works with a number of other BR locomotives and was withdrawn at the end of 1966 and cut up by Arnott Young of Parkgate.

41535, one of the second batch, was built at Derby Works and entered service in 1922. It was withdrawn, from Neath Court Sart, in September 1964 and scrapped by Bird's at Morriston soon afterwards. It is seen here at Gloucester on Saturday 4 January 1964. It appears to be missing its coupling rods. This was, perhaps, in preparation for imminent removal to Swansea East Dock where it was allocated for the next few months.

47000 sits inside its home shed, Derby on Sunday 12 May 1963. This was on the occasion of a visiting Warwickshire Railway Society special hauled by 34094 MORTEHOE which ran from Birmingham New Street to Derby Works and shed, Doncaster Works and shed and Barrow Hill shed. There were just ten locomotives in the same 0F class as 47000. It was one of the first five which were built by Kitson in 1932 (it had the works number 5644). It was withdrawn in October 1966 and scrapped at Cashmore's of Great Bridge.

47006 also inside Derby No.4 shed (actually a double roundhouse) on Sunday 12 May 1963. This was one of the second, later, batch of five 0F 0-4-0STs, constructed by British Railways at Horwich with greater coal capacity – it entered service in 1953. It was withdrawn in August 1966 and scrapped at Cashmore's of Great Bridge.

41734 has a break from shunting at Staveley Iron Works and rests on Staveley Barrow Hill shed on Sunday 12 May 1963. Several small tank engines were based there to fulfil an 1865 agreement whereby the Midland Railway would provide locomotives to work at the Staveley Coal and Iron Company works for one hundred years. This Johnson Midland Railway 1F 0-6-0T was built at Derby Works in 1884. It was withdrawn in December 1966 and cut up by Haselwood's of Attercliffe a few months later.

3F 0-6-0T 47236 in the shed yard at Carlisle Kingmoor on Sunday 12 July 1964. It was one of the sixty original Johnson '2441' class built for the Midland Railway by Vulcan Foundry. It entered service in 1902 and, like the rest, was later rebuilt with a Belpaire firebox. In this form the engines were the forerunners of the much more numerous LMS 'standard shunting tank' – collectively 'Jinties'. It was withdrawn the month after this photograph was taken. Many of the class were fitted with condensing apparatus to work in the London area but this one was not.

Jinty 47417, built at the Vulcan Foundry in 1926. This company constructed 120 of the 422 members of the class. Seen here at Gloucester Barnwood shed in April 1963, it had already been withdrawn, in the previous November. It was cut up in June. Do see *The Joy of Jinties*, recently published by Irwell Press.

Fowler 3F 0-6-0T 47629 at Derby on Sunday 12 May 1963. It had entered service in 1928 and was part of a batch of eighty-seven built by Beardmore of Dalmuir, Glasgow. It was one of the last three Jinties in BR service which were all withdrawn from Westhouses in October 1967, after working at the nearby Williamthorpe Colliery. There is a glimpse of a Derby-built Sultzer Type 2 (class 24) diesel behind.

3F 0-6-0T 47681, the last of the class to be built, entered service from Horwich in 1931. It was one of seven Jinties fitted with push-pull apparatus for passenger work at Swansea Upper Bank shed. It was shunting at Walton-on-the-Hill, Liverpool, on Tuesday 3 September 1963. Walton shed, where 47681 was based, closed three months later. 47681 was withdrawn in August 1965 and cut up at the end of the year by Cashmore's of Great Bridge.

47673 and 2-6-2T 41233 together on Llandudno Junction shed on Wednesday 30 June 1965. The 1932 built Jinty, one of only fifteen of this 422 strong class constructed by the LMS at Horwich, had been transferred from Mold Junction the month before. It was withdrawn in November 1966 and scrapped but lives on in the form of a Bachmann 00 scale model.

Carlisle Upperby's 47667 is busy about its station pilot duties at Carlisle Citadel on Sunday 12 July 1964. Both Carlisle sheds, Kingmoor and Upperby, provided Jinties for Citadel pilot work – often the same engines for several years, usually kept fairly presentable. Constructed at Horwich in 1931, 47667 was withdrawn from Skipton in November 1966 and scrapped by Ward's of Sheffield.

Drummond Caledonian Railway 264 class 0-4-0ST 56029 was built at St Rollox and entered service as 614 in 1895. It had already been withdrawn in December 1962 but was not cut up until August 1964, at Motherwell Machinery & Scrap at Wishaw,. It was languishing here with ex-North British Railway 0-6-0 64574 at a recently-closed Kipps shed on Saturday 24 August 1963.

McIntosh Caledonian Railway 782 class 3F 0-6-0T 56336 quietly rusting at Motherwell on Saturday 24 August 1963. Originally CR 609, it was built at St Rollox Works in 1910. It had already been withdrawn, in December 1962, and it was scrapped at the end of 1963 by Motherwell Machinery & Scrap of Wishaw.

55204 banished to the rear of Perth MPD (often indicative of imminent demise) on Tuesday 27 August 1963. This McIntosh 'Standard Passenger' 439 class 2P 0-4-4T was built at St Rollox in 1910 as CR 160. It became LMS 15204. It was withdrawn at the end of December 1962 and was cut up by Motherwell Machinery & Scrap of Wishaw a full two years later.

55269 too, is withdrawn at Perth on Tuesday 27 August 1963. It was one of ten 2P 0-4-4Ts developed from the McIntosh '439' class; built by Nasmyth Wilson, it entered service with the LMS in 1925 after the 1923 grouping. It was withdrawn in March 1962 and scrapped by Arnott Young of Troon three months after this photograph was taken.

6: Excursion Trains and Enthusiast Specials

Crewe North Class 5s 44683 and 44685 in the goods loop at Stratford-upon-Avon on Thursday 4 June 1964, on excursion 1X40 which had arrived from Glasgow. It was 07:45 in the morning and this must have been an overnight journey in both directions. I wonder if any of the passengers fell asleep in the theatre during the matinee performance of *Richard II* starring David Warner! Both locomotives were built by British Railways after Nationalisation at Horwich in 1950. 44683 was withdrawn in April 1968 and scrapped by Draper's of Hull. 44685 retired a year earlier, in April 1967, and met its end at Bird's, Morriston.

Class 5 44713 with green Southern Region coaching stock leaves Stratford-upon-Avon on the return leg of an excursion from Deal in Kent on the same day, Thursday 4 June 1964. It was ten past six in the afternoon so this was presumably after the matinee performance at the theatre. 44713, built at Horwich Works in 1948, was based at Northampton. It was a survivor because it was not withdrawn, from Lostock Hall, until the very last month of steam on British Railways; August 1968. It was cut up by Draper's of Hull.

Left. 53807 and 44558 run round the Home Counties Railway Society 'Somerset and Dorset' train at Highbridge to return to Evercreech Junction on Sunday 7 June 1964. The tour ran from Waterloo to Paddington via Bournemouth and Bath. 53807 and 44558 had taken over from 35005 CANADIAN PACIFIC at Bournemouth Central and would hand over to 7023 PENRICE CASTLE at Bath Green Park. 7025 SUDELEY CASTLE was also used later on this tour.

Below. A closer look at 44558 behind 53807 on the tour at Highbridge on Sunday 7 June 1964. It was built by Armstrong Whitworth and entered service as Somerset and Dorset Joint Railway 58 in 1922. It became LMSR 4558 in 1930, was withdrawn in December 1964 and scrapped by Cashmore's at Newport.

53807 and 44558 pause at Evercreech Junction on Sunday 7 June 1964. The 2-8-0 was built by Robert Stephenson and Hawthorn Ltd in 1925 as Somerset and Dorset Joint Railway 87. It became LMSR 9677 in 1930 and then 13807 in 1932. It was withdrawn from Bath Green Park in September 1964 and cut up by Cashmore's at Newport.

46251 CITY OF NOTTINGHAM rests for a while at Tebay station on the Stephenson Locomotive Society 'Pacific Pennine Three Summits Rail Tour' on Sunday 12 July 1964. This SLS special ran from Birmingham New Street over Shap to Carlisle and back via the Settle and Carlisle line and Leeds. 'Jubilee' 45647 STURDEE, 'Royal Scot' 46155 THE LANCER, and 'Coronation' 46255 CITY OF HEREFORD also provided motive power on this tour. The station, opened by the Lancaster and Carlisle Railway in 1852, closed in July 1968.

CITY OF NOTTINGHAM at Tebay that day. It was allocated to Crewe North at the time. It was withdrawn just three months after this tour, in October 1964, and scrapped by Cashmore's of Great Bridge. Tebay No.2 signal box can be seen in the distance with the line to Kirkby Stephen turning off to the right. This locomotive was unfortunately involved in a fatal accident at Winsford in Cheshire in April 1948 when, on a mail train, it ran into a passenger train.

46255 CITY OF HEREFORD pauses to take on water at Skipton on the 'Three Summits' tour on Sunday 12 July 1964. It had taken over from 46251 at Carlisle. Built at Crewe Works in 1946 and never streamlined, 46255 was allocated to Carlisle Kingmoor at the time. It was withdrawn just three months after this tour, in October 1964, and scrapped by Arnott Young at Troon.

Carrying a 55C Farnley Junction shed plate, 45647 STURDEE has just taken over from 46255 CITY OF HEREFORD at Leeds City on the tour. Named after the Admiral of the Fleet, Sir Frederick Charles Doveton Sturdee, it was built at Crewe and entered service in 1935. It was withdrawn in April 1967 and scrapped by Cashmore's at Great Bridge.

Crewe North's 46155 THE LANCER has replaced 45647 STURDEE at Crewe for the last leg to Birmingham New Street. It was built at Derby Works in 1930 and was taken out of service, from Kingmoor in December 1965, to be cut up by Arnott Young of Troon.

This is the view from the A422 Stratford-Banbury road bridge at Houndshill, 4F 44188 hauling the Stephenson Locomotive Society 'Farewell to the Stratford-upon-Avon and Midland Junction Railway' tour east in the sixty foot deep Goldicote Cutting, now a nature reserve, on Saturday 24 April 1965. The train had started from Birmingham Snow Hill double-headed with the now-preserved ex-GWR pannier tank 6435. 44188 hauled the train alone from Stratford Old Town to Woodford Halse and back.

Shortly afterwards 44188 crosses the Roman Fosse Way (which linked Exeter and Lincoln) at Fosse Bridge on Saturday 24 April 1965. The first coach is M26340M, an LMS 57ft third class brake (BTK). Regular freight workings had ceased eight weeks earlier and this was the last passenger train over the SMJR. Ten weeks later, in July, most of the line was officially closed leaving only the section from Fenny Compton to Burton Dassett as a branch serving the Ministry of Defence depot at Kineton.

44188, now near Kineton. After it returned to Stratford later that day, 44188 was joined by 6435 for the return run to Birmingham Snow Hill via Hatton. Allocated to Bescot, it was withdrawn seven months later, in November 1965, and scrapped by Cashmore's of Great Bridge.

'Crab' 42727 runs alongside rough seas at Pensarn with the Stephenson Locomotive Society (Midland Area) 'Farewell to GWR Locos & L&YR 2-6-0s' special from Birmingham Snow Hill on Sunday 27 March 1966. It hauled the train from Chester to Llandudno Junction and back.

42727 has just passed by at Pensarn with the special. This locomotive was built by the LMS at the ex Lancashire and Yorkshire Railway Horwich Works in 1927 and entered service as 13027. It was withdrawn, from Birkenhead (8H), in January 1967 and cut up later the same year by Cashmore's at Newport. 0-6-2T 6697 and Class 5 45250 were also used on this tour.

Banbury Class 5 44872 climbs Hatton Bank on a Ffestiniog Railway Society/Ian Allan special to the railway from Paddington on Saturday 30 April 1966. It had taken over from a diesel locomotive, Brush Type 4 (later class 47) D1744, at Banbury. Standard 4-6-0s 75020 and 75021 were in charge of the train later on the tour.

44872 gets on its way. It was withdrawn from Lostock Hall in September 1967 and cut up by J McWilliams at Shettlestone.

45073 and 45156 AYRSHIRE YEOMANRY approach the Chapel Lane bridge at Hoghton, between Blackburn and Lostock Hall, on the Severn Valley Railway Society/Manchester Rail Travel Society 'Farewell to BR Steam' special on Sunday 28 July 1968. The train ran from Birmingham New Street to Carnforth and Skipton and back with 48773, 70013 OLIVER CROMWELL, 75019 and 75027 also used on the tour.

45073 and 45156 a moment later, now passing under the Chapel Lane bridge. 45156 was not carrying its AYRSHIRE YEOMANRY nameplates that day.

Stanier Class 5 4-6-0s 44871 and 44894 cross the thirteen arch Robinwood (known by various names, like Knott Wood) Viaduct in the Calder Valley on train 1Z78 on Sunday 4 August 1968. This was the Stephenson Locomotive Society (Midland Area) 'Farewell to Steam No.1' special from Birmingham New Street which ran just one week before the official end of steam on British Railways. 44871 and 44894 were both constructed at Crewe Works in 1945 and withdrawn during the month the photograph was taken. 44894 was scrapped by Draper's of Hull but 44871 was bought directly for preservation from BR and has run on main line specials. The large building is Robinwood Mill.

British Railways standard 'Britannia' class Pacific 70013 OLIVER CROMWELL and Class 5 44781 cross Entwistle, also known as Armsgrove or Bradshaw Brook, Viaduct on train 1Z74 on Sunday 4 August 1968. Wayoh Reservoir is beyond. This special, the Locomotive Club of Great Britain 'The Last Day of Steam' rail tour, ran from London St Pancras to Manchester Victoria, Hellifield and Carnforth and back to London Euston. 45025, 45390, 48773, D63, D416 and E3064 were also used on the trip. 70013 was of course preserved at the end of steam as part of the National Collection, at first based at Bressingham in Norfolk. It was later restored to main line standards and has been used on special trains and on preserved railways.

Class 5 4-6-0 45110 is seen from the Mill Lane bridge as is runs through the two mile long, seventy foot deep Olive Mount Cutting, Liverpool, on the 'Fifteen Guinea Special' end of steam on BR train on Sunday 11 August 1968. The train, 1T57, ran from Liverpool Lime Street via Manchester Victoria and the Settle and Carlisle line to Carlisle and return. This was a fitting start for the route of the final steam run as ROCKET passed through the cutting on the opening day of the Liverpool and Manchester Railway on 15 September 1830.

45110 viewed this time from the A579 Winwick Lane overbridge near Kenyon Junction on the renowned 'Fifteen Guinea Special'. It was advertised as the last steam hauled train on British Railways on standard gauge track because the BR run Vale of Rheidol line was still steam worked. 45110 was built by the Vulcan Foundry in 1935 (works number 4653) and is now preserved on the Severn Valley Railway.

Nearing the end! 45110 heads towards Liverpool on the home stretch of the 'Fifteen Guinea Special'. It was 7:30 in the evening and thirty minutes later the officially last standard gauge British Railways steam-hauled train would arrive at Liverpool Lime Street. A sombre moment. BR brought in a steam ban the following day but fortunately it was not the last main line steam tour since the baton would later be passed on to preserved locomotives.

7 Irish Interlude

Ulster Transport Authority (UTA) No.91 THE BUSH, an ex LMS-Northern Counties Committee W Class two-cylinder 2-6-0, lets off steam on Adelaide shed, Belfast, on Tuesday 24 March 1964. There were fifteen in this class primarily intended for express passenger trains which was largely, it seems, a tender version of the LMS Fowler Class 4 2-6-4T. THE BUSH was one of the first batch of four which were fully constructed at the LMS Derby Works in 1933. The other eleven were assembled at Belfast York Road Works from parts supplied by Derby Works. THE BUSH was withdrawn in 1965. It had 6ft driving wheels at the Irish 5ft 3in gauge.

Known as 'Jeeps' to the railwaymen, the ex LMS-NCC Derby-produced WT class parallel boiler 2-6-4Ts were introduced in 1946. Eighteen examples of this tank engine version of the 2-6-0 Ws were built, first by the LMS when George Ivatt was Chief Mechanical Engineer and then, after it was nationalised, by British Railways. 54, a BR 1950 product, was on Adelaide shed, Belfast, on Friday 6 September 1963. It was withdrawn in February 1970.

A WT waits to remove a goods van from a morning train from Belfast at Portadown station on Wednesday 25 March 1964. The carriage, n312, was ex GNR(I) K7 type corridor 'tea car' No.41 built in 1914 but converted to fully third class seating in 1948. The 12-ton goods van, No.2408, was a ex-LMS-NCC 2400 type fitted vehicle. These were often attached to passenger trains to convey parcels. The roof of the signal box situated at the end of the island platform can be seen behind the van.

WT 2-6-4T 56 leaves Portadown on Wednesday 25 March 1964 at the head of the cross-border 09:15 Dublin Amiens Street (now Connolly) station to Belfast Great Victoria Street station, where it was due to arrive at 12:25. Portadown station can be seen in the background as can the tower of Saint Mark's Church which was rebuilt in 1928 as a war memorial to those killed in the First World War. 56 was built at Derby in 1950 and withdrawn in 1970. The locomotive would almost certainly have followed the practice of the day and taken over this train from a *Córas Iompair Éireann* diesel locomotive at Dundalk. I have since learned, thanks to Anthony Gray and Joe Cassells, that the signals are the Portadown advance starter and the Seagoe down distant.

LMS-NCC 13X shunting at Belfast Docks Donegall Quay alongside the Heysham shed on Friday 6 September 1963. It was one of three V Class 0-6-0 goods locomotives built at Derby Works in 1923; it was rebuilt as a Class VI with a Belpaire firebox and new boiler at York Road Works, Belfast, in 1953. The horse-drawn flat wagon belonged to John Harkness and Co which also dealt with heavy haulage and at one time had traction engines in its fleet.

13X still shunting at Belfast Docks on Friday 6 September 1963. The V Class had 5ft 2½in diameter driving wheels and 19in×24in inside cylinders. The 2,090 gallon capacity six wheeled tender is particularly interesting for its outside springing, already obsolete in 1923. The suffix X indicated the locomotive was restricted to shunting duties and would not be overhauled. At the time of the photograph it was the sole survivor of its class and it was officially withdrawn in August the following year but I saw it, clearly out of action without its tender, at York Road shed in the March and I doubt if it ever worked again.

8: Early Preservation

Preserved Midland Railway Compound 1000 prepares to leave the Stratford-upon-Avon and Midland Junction Railway line at Stratford on a Gloucestershire Railway Society special on Saturday 27 May 1961. It carried the code 1X06 and was hauling seven coaches. It had arrived much too late for colour film of the speed of the time but it still looked good in the twilight. The tour took a roundabout route from Gloucester Eastgate to Alcester, Derby, Loughborough Midland Road, Oakham, Wellingborough, Northampton Castle, Towcester, Fenny Compton, Stratford, Honeybourne and back to Gloucester Eastgate. 1000 was built at Derby Works in 1902, re-built in 1914 and withdrawn from regular service in September 1951.

Above. One of a class of thirty 0-6-0Ts built at Bow Works, North London Railway 116 entered service in 1899. In 1909 it became LNWR 2650 and at the grouping LMS 2505 and later 27505. It was withdrawn as BR 58850 in September 1960 from Rowsley shed after working on the Cromford and High Peak line, a long way from East London. This is Sheffield Park on the Bluebell Railway with the engine in its LNWR guise as 2650 on Saturday 28 April 1962. Trains at the time were 'topped and tailed' with a locomotive at each end as they were not allowed into Horsted Keynes until later in the year and there were no run round facilities at the temporary terminus at Bluebell Halt. The carriage, part of the Metropolitan Railway 'Chesham' set, is brake third No.307 with ventilators added in 1907-8 and since removed when the set was fully restored.

Right. LNWR Webb 0-6-2T 1054 was built at Crewe Works in 1888. It became LMS 7799, later 27799, and BR 58926. Just before it was withdrawn, in October 1958, it had been used as a temporary replacement for the stationary boiler at Pontypool Road which was under repair. It was saved for preservation and moved, after a repaint into LNWR livery at Crewe, to the Railway Preservation Society at Hednesford where it is seen in this photograph on 24 March 1963. Shortly after this it was donated to the National Trust and moved to Penrhyn Castle in North Wales. It later went to the Dinting Railway Centre and it featured in the 1980 150th anniversary events of the Liverpool and Manchester Railway. Now based on the Keighley and Worth Valley Railway, it has visited a number of other preserved lines.

PRINCE, an L&Y 'Pug' 0-4-0ST at the United Glass Charlton Works on Wednesday 8 January 1964. It became LMS 11243 but was withdrawn in 1931 and sold to John Mowlem & Co Ltd, a contractor, where it was given the name BASSETT. It was then bought by the United Glass Bottle Company in 1933 and named PRINCE. It was sold to the Lancashire & Yorkshire Railway Preservation Society early in 1967 and is one of only two of the fifty-seven strong Horwich-built L&YR 'class 21', nicknamed 'Pugs', to have survived into preservation. It is now to be found at the Ribble Steam Railway at Preston.

Ivatt 2MT 2-6-2T 41298 at a Longmoor Military Railway open day, Saturday 8 June 1968. It spent all its BR working life on the Southern Region until withdrawn from Nine Elms in July 1967. It was bought for preservation by the Ivatt Trust and based at Longmoor until the place closed; it moved to the Quainton Railway Society site but it is now to be found on the Isle of Wight Steam Railway.

Highland Railway 103 on the Stephenson Locomotive Society (Scottish Area) and Branch Line Society 'Scottish Rambler No.4', which ran over four days with different locomotives, passing through Paisley St James station on Saturday 17 April 1965. The train had started from Glasgow at the now closed St Enoch terminus. It ran along a number of local lines including those to East Kilbride, Greenock Princes Pier and Renfrew Wharf, visiting Paisley's numerous stations and goods lines five times! Paisley St James station was opened in 1841 by the Glasgow, Paisley and Greenock Railway which was later absorbed into the Caledonian Railway.

103 catches the evening light on a Branch Line Society special near Abington on the West Coast main line on Sunday 17 October 1965. This train ran from Glasgow Central station to Dumfries via Kilmarnock and then returned via Lockerbie and Carstairs. HR 103 is a 4-6-0 built in 1894 by Sharp, Stewart & Co. one of fifteen designed by David Jones for the Highland Railway intended mainly for freight trains. It was withdrawn from service as LMSR 17916 in 1934 and was preserved. In 1959 it was restored to working order in Highland Railway livery for use over a few years on special trains. Starring in *Those Magnificent Men in their Flying Machines* it was the last steam engine to use Bedford shed, in May 1964. It is now exhibited at the Riverside Museum, Glasgow.

Caledonian Railway 123 waiting, appropriately, on the old CR Dalry Road shed in Edinburgh before heading aforementioned 'The Scottish Rambler No.4' railtour, this time on Easter Monday 19 April 1965. This ran between Edinburgh Princess Street station, just five months before it closed, and Carstairs. The impressive neo-Gothic building seen behind the shed on the right is Donaldson's Hospital designed by the architect William Henry Playfair and built in 1851. Formerly the School for the Deaf, it has now been converted into flats.

123 alongside the shed building that same day. Dalry Road closed in the October only six months after this photograph was taken. Edinburgh Castle is just visible in the distance beyond the tender. CR 123, a 'single' with 7ft driving wheels, was exhibited at the Edinburgh International Exhibition of 1886 where it won a gold medal.

123 a little later that day, Easter Monday 19 April 1965, near Auchengray on the ex-Caledonian line between Edinburgh and Carstairs. It was hauling two restored CR carriages on the 'Rambler No.4'. 123 had been withdrawn in 1935 as LMSR 14010 and preserved. In 1959 it was restored to working order in Caledonian Railway livery for use on special trains and, like HR 103, it is now exhibited at the Riverside Museum, Glasgow.

46201 PRINCESS ELIZABETH at the Dowty Railway Preservation Society's premises at Ashchurch on 19 July 1964. Withdrawn in October 1962, it was bought by the Princess Elizabeth Locomotive Society which kept it here; it later moved to the Bulmers Railway Centre in Hereford.

Steam on the main line only a year after the BR ban? PRINCESS ELIZABETH, now as LMS 6201, with 7808 COOKHAM MANOR and 0-6-2T 6697, pass by at Bishopton, near Stratford-upon-Avon, hauled by a Class 47 diesel on their way from Dowty's to a Tyseley Open Day on Saturday 27 September 1969.

6201 PRINCESS ELIZABETH passing Tyseley station in glorious sunshine during the open day on Sunday 28 September 1969. It was carrying a 27A, Glasgow Polmadie, shed plate which was its allocation soon after it was built in 1933. In April 1976 it left Ashchurch for its new base at Bulmer's in Hereford. When that closed it was moved to the Midland Railway Centre at Butterley. It has since been at Crewe, Tyseley, Southall and, at present, Carnforth and has been used on a number of main line steam special trains and even, in 2012, a Royal Train.

46235 CITY OF BIRMINGHAM in front of the art deco Colonial Mutual Life Assurance building on Great Charles Street while being delivered to the Birmingham Science Museum in Newhall Street on Sunday 22 May 1966. Robert Wynn & Sons Ltd of Newport's heavy duty prime mover with the number plate GDW 277 was named DREADNOUGHT and was built during the second world war by the Pacific Car & Foundry Company in Renton in Washington State. It was one of six bought by Wynn's as war surplus.

46235 CITY OF BIRMINGHAM moves off on the way to the Birmingham Science Museum on Sunday 22 May 1966. It was built, streamlined, in 1939 but the casing was removed in 1946. It had been withdrawn from service at the end of September 1964.

46235 CITY OF BIRMINGHAM is in place at the Birmingham Science Museum in Newhall Street on Wednesday 12 October 1966. The building has yet to be erected around it! When the museum closed 46235 was moved to the new Thinktank Science Museum at Millennium Point, near to Curzon Street station.

5593 KOLHAPUR working short shuttle trains from the depot to alongside the main line at the Tyseley open day on Sunday 4 May 1969. CLUN CASTLE and two Black Five 4-6-0 locomotives were also in attendance and FLYING SCOTSMAN visited on an enthusiast special.

The following year KOLHAPUR is on the shuttle trains at another Tyseley open day, on Sunday 17 May 1970. It was built by the North British Locomotive Company in 1934 and was withdrawn, from Leeds Holbeck, in October 1967 and bought directly from BR by the Standard Gauge Steam Trust. It has been used on main line tours and is based at Tyseley.

On Saturday 31 August 1968, Ivatt 2MT 2-6-0 46443 waits to leave Bridgnorth on a train for Hampton Loade. This was an open day for 'day members' that pre-dated the Severn Valley Light Railway Order granted in November 1969. 3205 and 43106 were also in steam that day.

43106 approaches Eardington on that open day, Saturday 31 August 1968. It is the last survivor of 162 Ivatt class 4 2-6-0s; withdrawn in June 1968 it was chosen for preservation by the Ivatt Class 4 Group and moved to the SVR where it remains still. This open day was at the end of the very month that saw the 11 August 'Fifteen Guinea Special'.